Vincenzo Cardarelli: The Forgotten amongst the Great

A Collection of the Best Poems Translated in English

Alessandro Baruffi

First Printing: 2015
ISBN: 9781520485812

Publisher:
LiteraryJoint Press, Philadelphia, PA (USA)
www.literaryjoint.com

Ordering information for U.S. and non-U.S. trade bookstores and wholesalers: special discounts are available on quantity purchases by corporations, associations, educators, and others. For details, contact the publisher at the above listed address.

Cover image: Portrait of Vincenzo Cardarelli, by Amerigo Bartoli, 1934, Galleria Civica d'Arte Moderna, Turin.

Vincenzo Cardarelli (pseudonym of Nazareno Caldarelli, 1887-1959) journalist, poet, and literary critic, led a solitary, dignified existence, from a humble background, through self-taught education and innumerable peregrinations, until his final days in poverty and loneliness. He stood and sought for all that a true artist and intellectual has to stand and seek for: the uncompromising authenticity of art.

Table of Contents:

Contemplations

A Few Forewords from the Translator

Until now, with the sole exception of a few poems translated by the great Irish poet Desmond O'Grady in the late 1950's, the work of Vincenzo Cardarelli had remained precluded to the English speaking world and the international audience at large. It is my sincere hope that the publication of this extensive collection will finally disclose the doors to one of the most prominent, yet still relatively unexplored, Italian and European poet of the twentieth century.

The poetry of Vincenzo Cardarelli encompasses 1910's avant-garde and 1920's restoration period, revolving around two main literary experiences which stood like pillars supporting the bridge of his artistic expression: the collaboration with the literary magazine "La Voce" (The Voice), close to the avant-guard (linguistic expressionism, irrationalism, and decadent movements) and the conservative publication "La Ronda" (The Patrol), of which Cardarelli was one of the founders, close to classicism (cult of the past, formalism, and the recuperation of the traditional role of intellectuals in society).

Yet, the greatness of Cardarelli's poetical journey goes far beyond any formal classification or ideology, as it delves into a diversity of universal, immortal themes, such as uprootedness and loss of identity, metaphorical travels, the laborious work of memory and passing of time and seasons, and the contemplation of nature and beauty.

Barcelona, Catalonia, May 2015

The Seasons

October (Ottobre)

Once, it was in Summer,
it was at that fire, at those ardors,
that my imagination awakened.
I incline now towards Autumn
of a color that raptures;
I love the tired season
which has already harvested the grapes.
No other thing resembles me more,
nothing consoles me more,
than this air that odors
of must and wine,
of this old sun of October
shining in the plundered vineyards.

Unexpected Autumn sun,
shining as in a beyond world,
with tender perdition
and vagabond happiness,
you find us exhausted,

braced for the worst and with sorrowful souls.
This is precisely why we cherish you,
vague, surviving sun:
you know not how to bid us farewell
coming back every morning
like a renewed miracle,
the prettier the more you fade
and are about to expire.
And with these stunning days
you compose your own season
which is thoroughly a sweet agony.

From the collection "Poesie," 1942, by Vincenzo Cardarelli.

Autumn (Autunno)

Autumn. We felt its coming
in the wind of August,
in the rains of September
torrential and weeping
and a shiver ran through the earth
which now, bare and sad,
welcomes a bewildered sun.
Now passes and declines,
in this Autumn progressing
with unspeakable slowness,
the best time of our life
and lengthily bids us farewell.

From the Collection "Poesie," 1949, by Vincenzo Cardarelli.

Trick (Scherzo)

The wood in Springtime
has a soul, a voice.
It is the singing of the cuckoo full of air,
that sounds as blown through a flute.
Inside the recall, softer
than the deceiving echo,
we proceed in delusion:
The chestnut tree is light green.
Even the ancient brooms
are oozing.
Around the shady tree trunks,
amidst the playful sunbeams,
are dancing the hamadryads.(*)

From the Collection"Poesie," 1942, by Vincenzo Cardarelli.

(*) Wood nymphs. In Greek and Roman Mythology, a wood nymph who lives only as long as the tree of which she is the spirit lives. From [Middle English amadriad,

from Latin Hamadryas, Hamadryad-, from Greek Hamadruas : hama, together with; see sem- in Indo-European roots + Druas, dryad (from drūs, oak; see deru- in Indo-European roots).] American Heritage® Dictionary of the English Language, Fifth Edition.

February (Febbraio)

February is lighthearted.
It does not possess the restful times of great Winter,
it has the pinpricks,
the tricks of a Spring about to be born.
From February's Bora wind
tranquility you shall not expect.
This month is a boy,
pesky and provoking,
which turns the house upside-down,
stirs the blood, announces the foolery of March,

perilous and mutant.

From the collection "Poesie," 1936, by Vincenzo Cardarelli.

Marzo (Marzo)

Today, Spring
is an effervescent wine.
Like a foam is the first green
on the great elms's bloomed wisps
where the seeds already falls
like diffuse rain.
Amongst the brimful and prodigal
branches,
a goldfinch is pecking.
Green window shutters flash
on red facades
which the clear, merry wind
of March is cleaning.
All is a color of fields.
The ivy too is deluded,
the moss is greener
on the old, oblivious logs
which have no season.
Shaken by an immense breath
the city lives a day

of country humors.
Inebriated, springtime
runs in the blood.

From the collection "Poesie," 1936, by Vincenzo Cardarelli.

April (Aprile)

So many tired words
come to my mind
in this rainy day of April
when the barnyard is like a crushed
cloud
or a flower that is spoiling.
Within a veil of rain
all is dressed like new.
The humid and dear earth
stings me and melts me away.
If your eyes are boggy and black
like hell,
then my sorrow is fresh
like a runlet.

From the collection "Poesie," 1936, by Vincenzo Cardarelli.

Summery (Estiva)

Outspread Summer,
season of dense climates
of great mornings
of dawns with no noise,
one wakes up like in an aquarium
of identical days, astral,
season the least prone
to obscurity and crises,
happiness of spaces,
no earthly promise
can give peace to my heart
as much as the certainty of a sun
that is spilling over your sky,
extreme season, which lays
down in enormous restful times,
offering gold to the greatest of dreams,
season which allows the light
to over-stretch time
beyond the boundaries of the day,
and seemingly puts everything

in the order that precedes
some of the cadences of eternal awaiting.

From the collection "Poesie," 1936, by Vincenzo Cardarelli.

October Mornings (Mattini d'ottobre)

Day by day the sun
is turning paler and paler.
It is a pallor that unnerves us
and saddens a soul:
an agony of light that is dimming,
a sigh that slowly is dying away.
In such October mornings
as I wander in the midst of a throng
I go on like a shadow that might fall
without any noise,
relishing the Autumn sun
which is the pale sun of long death.

From the collection "Poesie Aggiunte," 1949,
by Vincenzo Cardarelli.

November (Novembre)

There is a day when all the ants exit the wood
to make their bundle for the Winter.
Soon afterwards, come the long autumnal rains,
similar to a great pouring cry, endless.
It is a cry gushing out like rivers, torrents,
that swells the lake, plows the
streets, ruins
bridges and floods over the fields, obstinately green.
The walls cover themselves
with velveteen.
When no one expects it anymore, a chilly sun,
more precious than old gold, is back every morning,
to visit the acacia's leafs

which are still dripping on the window-
sills,
the dry leaves of the the plane trees
that the wind sweeps along the drive-
ways.

From the collection "Opere Complete," 1962, by Vincenzo Cardarelli.

Eternal Places

Sardinia (Sardegna)

Against the languid sky are engraved,
oh Sardinia, your mountains of iron.
A sky that seems as if veiled
by a sickly
pollen, to look at which one is tantalized.
Melancholic Circe,
it is through this recall
that you keep one from leaving,
and standing by the nostalgic mount
Limbara.
And it is so that a Sardinian
can never betray his faithful land.

When the cistus no longer scents
and through the ways of the seas,
a message of the mysterious life
that within you is hidden,
the partridge is trustingly nearing,
I traveled, oh Sardinia, your saline
roads of Gallura,

the land of Orosei, white, African,
the granitic and wooded Barbagia,
the red Ogliastra region,
and beyond the Campidano plain, whose
women
have bosoms made of stone,

I went further to Teulada,
where fallow deers would prance
on the doorsteps of the host's house.
I stopped amongst the shady
orange groves of Milis. I went up
the windy plateau, towards Mandas,
accompanied by a soldier's song,
the only medicine
for such a melancholy.
And on the course of an assiduous and
glad river
I found myself amongst your proud folks
of Barbagia,
who from the Gennargentu Mountains,
where against the white granite
leaf oaks and black ilexes,

once used to came down
to the fertile and muddy plain land.
So that from the mountain to the flat
I ventured, through large paradises
of game
and lands so lonely that by going across
them
any simple rider is a knight.
I have come to know you everywhere,
ardent and varied island,
with your customs, your hieratic chants.
And already Summer along the dry
pebbly shores
turned the oleander white,
while on the mountains persisted
an inexpressible color
of an island Springtime.
And on your virgin earth emerged
here and there, solicitous,
the first, rough relics of man
which turns you heavy and sullen in so
much light.
Fabulous journey
which I made again in a heartbeat,

withdrawing into the evening,
when already you were no other
than a dreamy sky
on the edge of a mountain.

Land of strong wines,
nation of ancient shepherds
and warm women,
flower of the Mediterranean,
bloomed in the time when all was enclo-
sed
within our sea,
you carry within you the scent
of a courteous and adventurous century.
I perceived this in the grace
of your language,
in the winds that you breathe.
And I saw Pisa,
where at once on the alpine hilltop
two castle's old stone walls, horrendous,
recollect of Earl Ugolino.
Yet, tell me what name, if not Rome's,
sends flashes through the eye
of your shepherd.

From the collection "Poesie," 1936, by Vincenzo Cardarelli.

Evening of Gavinana (Sera di Gavinana)

Here is the evening and the rain stops
on the Tuscan Apennines.
As the clouds descend to the valley,
huddled here and there
like mist nests amongst the intricate trees,
the mountains grow purple in color.
A sweet wandering then
to whom during the day toils
and in himself, in disbelief, wallows.
From the busy hamlets, here below,
comes
a glad and thick jabber in which
one perceives the declining day
and the imminent rest.
Mingled with it is the throbbing, the high
and dry
pounding of the truck on the wide
white road that crosses the mountains.
And everything in the evening,

crickets, church bells, springs,
becomes a concert and a prayer,
trembles in the clear air.
And how shiner is,
in the hour that has no other light,
the blanket of your hips, Apennines.
On your fields that climb in wide turns,
this green liquid, that peeks again
amongst the sun's deceits at every downpour,
to the wind it changes colors, and enraptures me,
along the restless path,
and tenderly hushes
the vagabond soul.

From the collection "Poesie," 1936, by Vincenzo Cardarelli.

Venetian Autumn (Autunno veneziano)

Upon me is the humid and cold breath
of autumnal Venice.
Now that Summer,
sultry and touched by Sirocco,
like magic has gone,
a stern moon of September
shines, full of dire forebode,
on the city of waters and stones
which reveals her features of Gorgon,
contagious and wicked.
Dead is the silence of the canals which
reek,
under the watery moon,
in any one of them seems to
rest the corpse of Ophelia:
tombs covered with rotten flowers
and other green wastes,
where passes by, with a swash,
the ghost of the gondolier.

Oh Venetian nights,
without the crow of roosters,
without voices of fountains,
somber laguna-nights,
that no tender whisper soothes,
sinister houses, jealous,
vertical on the canals,
asleep without breath,
you weigh on my heart more than ever.
Here, no impetuous and funereal winds
of a September in the mountains,
no odor of grapes's harvest, no wash-
basins
of tearful rains,
no crash of leaves that fall.
A tussock that turns yellow and dies
on a window's ledge
is all it is a Venetian Autumn.

Thus, in Venice seasons are delirious.

Throughout her fields of marble and her
canals
all is but disoriented lights,

lights which dream of a good earth
that is fragrant and fruitful.
Only a winter shipwreck convenes
to this city which lives not,
which blooms not,
other than like a ship does in the bottom
of the sea.

From the collection "Poesie," 1942, by Vincenzo Cardarelli.

Night Landscape (Paesaggio notturno)

It lies up there my childhood.
There upon that hill
that I see again at night,
passing by on the railway,
marked by bright lights.
Smell of burnt stubble
strikes me at the station.
Ancient and diffuse smell
similar to many voices calling me.
But the train flees. I go, not knowing
where.
My company is a friend
who is not even awake.
No one thinks or guesses
what it means to me
this motherly land which I overfly
like a stranger, like a betrayer.

From the collection "Prologhi," 1916, by Vincenzo Cardarelli.

September in Venice (Settembre a Venezia)

Already by September darken
in Venice the precocious sunsets
and the stones dress in mourning.
The sun's last beam is a dart
on the golden mosaics and lights up
fires made of straw, ephemeral beauty.
And quietly, behind the Procuratìe, (*)
meanwhile rises the moon.
The festive and silver lights laugh,
they keep chatting afar with trepidation
in the cool and dark air.
I look at them in fascination.
Perhaps, later on I will remember
these great nights
that are quick to come,
and their lights
that now sink me a bit into despair
(to me, always estrange and distant!)

more beautiful and livelier
will shine back again
in my imagination.
And it will be a true and quiet
happiness mine.

From the collection "Poesie," 1936, by Vincenzo Cardarelli.

(*) Literally "procuracies," they are three connected buildings on St Mark's Square in Venice. They are also connected to St Mark's Clocktower.

Evening of Liguria (Sera di Liguria)

Slow and rosy up from the sea rises
the evening of Liguria, perdition
of loving hearts and far away things.
In the gardens the couples linger,
one by one the windows light up
like many theaters.
Buried in the fog the sea exhales its scent.
The churches on the coastline resemble
boats
that are about to set sail.

From the collection "Opere Complete," 1962, by Vincenzo Cardarelli.

Liguria (Liguria)

Liguria is a graceful land.
The burning rock, the polished clay
quicken with the wine leaves in the sun.
The olive tree is a giant. At springtime
everywhere the ephemeral mimosa ap-
pears.
Shadow and sun perform in succession
along those deep valleys
which hide from the sea,
along the paved roads
that climb up, through fields of roses
wells and parceled lands,
skirting farms and walled vineyards.
In that arid land the sun crawls
upon the stones like a serpent.
There are days when the sea
is a garden in full bloom.
Messages are borne in the wind.
Venus is once again born

by the gusts of the mistral.
Oh churches of Liguria, like ships
about to be launched!
Open to the winds and waves
Ligurian graveyards!
A red sadness colors you
when in the evening, similar to a flower
that is wilting, the great light
fades away and dies.

From the collection "Poesie," 1936, by Vincenzo Cardarelli.

Contemplations

Ruthless Memory (Memoria spietata)

Oh, ruthless memory, what have you done
of my village?
A village of ghosts
where nothing has changed but the living beings
that usurp the place of the dead.
Here all stands still, enchanted,
in my remembrance.
Even the wind.
How many times, oh place of my birth,
within you I came to seek
what belongs to me most and I have lost.
That ancient wind, those ancient voices,
and the odors and the seasons
of a time, alas, already lived.

From the collection "Opere Complete," 1962, by Vincenzo Cardarelli.

Past (Passato)

Our memories, these exceedingly long shadows
of our brief body,
this tail of death
that we leave behind as we live,
the dreadful and lasting memories,
here they appear already:
melancholic and mute
ghosts agitated by a funereal wind.
And by now you are nothing more than a memory.
Your are well past and gone in my memory.
Yes, now I can say that
you belong to me
and something between us had happened
irrevocably.
All ended, taken away!

Precipitous and gentle
our time caught up with us.
Made of fleeting moments, it has woven
a circled and sad story.
We ought to have known that love
burns life and gives time flying wings.

From the collection "Poesie," 1942, by Vincenzo Cardarelli.

A Front-light (Un fanale)

One Winter evening
I saw a front-light at Mount Savello,
shining in the fog.
It was an unexpected bus.
It was, that light, a great promise
to a city of bums,
howling its own struggles,
martyred by the infamous war.
It was the future that bloomed again
in thousands of beings
around myself, desperate, concluded.
And solitary, I was going,
saying to myself:
the day runs to the evening
like life to death.
Now is close the sunset.
And you will be able to take refuge
in that night to which no dawn follows.

From the collection "Poesie Aggiunte," 1949, by Vincenzo Cardarelli.

Abandonment (Abbandono)

You flew away
like a dove
and got lost yonder, to the East.
Yet remained the places that saw you
and the hours of our encounters.
Deserted hours,
places that to me became a sepulcher
of which I am the guardian.

From the collection "Poesie," 1936, by Vincenzo Cardarelli.

Seagulls (Gabbiani)

I know not where seagulls make their
nest
where find they peace.
I am like them
in perpetual flight.
I skim life
like they do with the water catching food.
And perhaps like them too, I cherish
quietness,
the great quietness of the sea,
but my fate is to live
wavering in the gale.

From the collection "Poesie," 1942, by Vincenzo Cardarelli.

Nostalgia (Nostalgia)

High on cliffs
beaten by winds,
is a leafy cemetery:
a Christian oasis in Tatar's Etruria.
Down there is the gorgeous
young woman of the Velchas, (*)
who still lives in the Tomb of the Orcus.
It is the gentle bed
of the Girl
just nearby.
Legions of dead descended
into that ancient earth where I hoped
to sleep one day and grow roots.
Oh, to be able to bury
in the silent city
together with myself the fable
of my life!
Not to be else than a corroded stone,
a name that is canceled,

and sleep without memory in the womb
of the homeland as if I had never
been separated from it.
Yet in the extreme gasp
I might be deluded.
I will die when and where
the fate wants.
Perhaps, better befits the vagrant,
who left the fatherly dwelling fall behind,
to be dispersed.
And that to his tantalized bones remains
the yearning, the desire of return.

From the collection "Poesie," 1949, by Vincenzo Cardarelli.

(*) The Tomb of Orcus (Italian: Tomba dell'Orco), sometimes called the Tomb of Murina (Italian: Tomba dei Murina) is a 4th-century BC Etruscan hypogeum (burial chamber) in Tarquinia, Italy. Discovered in 1868, it displays Hellenistic influences in its remarkable murals, which include the portrait of Velia Velcha, an Etruscan noblewoman, and the only known pictorial representation of the demon Tuchulcha. In general, the murals are

noted for their depiction of death, evil, and unhappiness.

Because the tomb was built in two sections at two stages, it is sometimes referred to as the Tombs of Orcus I and II; it is believed to have belonged to the Murina family, an offshoot of the Etruscan Spurinnae. The foundation is inscribed with the following enigmatic phrase:

"LARΘIALE HVLXNIESI MARCESIC CALIAΘESI MVNSLE NACNVAIASI ΘAMCE LE..."

To Death (Alla morte)

Dying, yes,
not to be assaulted by death !
Dying, persuaded
that such a journey is the best.
And in that ultimate instant to be cheer-
ful
like when one counts the minutes
of the wall clock at the station
and each of them is worth a century.
For death is the faithful spouse
that takes over the deceitful mistress,
we do not want to receive her as an in-
truder,
nor run away with her.
Too many a time we departed
without a goodbye!
On the verge of stepping, in a moment,
into the time
when even our memory

will desert us,
let us, oh Death, bid farewell to the world,
allow us to linger a moment.
The incommensurable step ought not be precipitous.
The sheer thought of a sudden death
freezes my very blood.
Oh Death, do not clutch me away
rather announce yourself from afar
and, as a friend, take me
like the ultimate of my habitudes.

From the collection "Poesie," 1942, by Vincenzo Cardarelli.

Friendship (Amicizia)

We do not know each other. I think of those days
when, lost in time, we met,
of our regrettable intimacy.
We have always left each other
without goodbyes,
with regrets and excuses from far away.
We indeed respected each other at pace,
cautious beasts,
skilled hunters,
to act laboriously
our roles of strangers.
Despairing shyness,
dizzy and insurmountable pauses.
spoke, in our secrets,
of the avoided contact and vain enchantment.
Something has always remained with us,
bitter vaunt

not to have caved in to our own abandonments,
something we have always missed.

From the collection "Poesie," 1942, by Vincenzo Cardarelli.

Deluded Youth (Illusa gioventù)

Oh youth, innocence, illusions,
time with no sin, golden age!
After you are past and gone
one uses to regret you
as a lost treasure.
I do know that you were a misfortune.
I know that fire you were not, rather ice,
oh my candid, boyish faiths,
beneath whose mantle I lived
like a tree trunk buried under the snow:
a green, mossy trunk,
rich in sap and sterile.
Now that, exhausted and gnawed,
having let loose of you, in a heartbeat I traveled
my blooming seasons
and I see scattered on the ground
the small fruit they yielded,
now that my fate I have known,
whichever that is I ask not. So rapidly

flees away life that any fate is fine
for such a brief day.
My only regret is you, oh early deceits.

From the collection "Poesie," 1936, by Vincenzo Cardarelli.

To Someone About to Leave (A un partente)

You will migrate, oh friend
from the Italian rubbles
towards the intact, idyllic Helvetia.
Light, like that of swallows,
shall be your flight.
And like a swallow you shall cross over
high up, above the flames,
which make the sky an inferno.
Higher than death, which above us,
doomed ancients,
will keep standing.

We called upon her, it is in her good right
to claim us.
But the guest who, born in
an innocent land,
came to suffer, guiltless,
from our woes,
it is fair for him to leave and deprive us
of his undeserved goodness.
Our heart follows you, oh friend.
The best wish of those who remain ac-
companies you in the audacious passage.

From the collection "Poesie," 1942, by Vincenzo Cardarelli.

Adrift (Alla deriva)

I myself have punished life by living it.
Till where my heart could bear
I boldly ventured.
Now my day is no else
than a sterile repetition
of ill habits
and I wish I could set free from the black circle.
Once I make it to dawn,
a fancy takes hold of me, a craving
of not to sleep.
And I dream absurd departures,
impossible liberations.
Alas. All my enclosed
and burning remorse
has no other easement
than sleep, when it comes.
In vain, in vain strive I
to possess the days
that overwhelm me noisily.

I myself drown in time.

From the collection "Poesie," 1942, by Vincenzo Cardarelli.

Times Change (Tempo che muta)

Just as the colors of
seasons change,
so do the moods and thoughts of men.
All in the world is but fickle time.
And here is already the pallid,
sepulchral Autumn,
while just yesterday was reigning
a flourishing, almost eternal, Summer.

From the collection "Poesie," 1936, by Vincenzo Cardarelli.

Reflections upon Love and Beauty

Maternity (Maternità)

Poor woman with turgid breasts,
your only wealth
is your milk.
And how much of it have you lavished,
those days of a Summer that is almost de-
funct,
to your florid child.
With unexhausted vein you nourished
him,
glad to bloom again
in his blooming.
At the slightest snivel was the bosom ex-
posed
free and bare with chaste easiness.
Albeit not pretty, you felt
healthy and attractive in the cheerful
mystery:
the baby was shaping himself,
mother and son were growing together.

It is so that for you a whole Summer passed by.
Now the Autumn wind mortifies you.
Sorrowful is your appearance,
helpless mother,
indigent bearer,
until now so oblivious.
What crosses your mind?
Is it melancholy for the accomplished work
or the black cortege
of miseries and woes
drawing nearer, that is turning mournful your face?

From the collection "Poesie," 1942, by Vincenzo Cardarelli.

Idyll (Idillio)

Through a shaded dirt track
between two walls of rusty stones
from which sunbathed grape leaves
sprouted up,
I saw one day, in Liguria,
(oh unexpected encounter!)
a young country girl
standing upright on the edge of her vi-
neyard.
Solitary was the path,
ardent the time of the day.
She looked at me, and smiled,
the lassie.
And I told her, drawing near,
words that I heard rising
from the blood,
from my whole being, in praise
of her beauty.
Beneath the blush of her face beaded

with perspiration from her paused toil
her mouth was laughing brightly.
She was barefoot. A chip
of golden clay
dressed her feet accustomed to daily
bathing at the spring.
Her eyes, fiery and shiny,
were glimmering with youth,
shiny and profound.
And behind her, so earthy and splendid,
the well known and trusty shades
of the familiar grape tree
seemed to watch over her.
All was peace around
and rustic silence.

From the collection "Poesie," 1936, by Vincenzo Cardarelli.

Encounter on the Tramway (Incontro in circolare)

Tall, brunette, strong hips,
beneath a unpretentious coat,
the pretty girl confused
amongst the wretched crowd
of an inner ring's tramway car,
appeared wholly free from any trouble.
Standing on the corridor, keeping slightly apart,
her legs like those of a statue
withstood any bump
as a solid bridge on a swollen river.
Not glory through her was revealed,
not frenzy of life or youth,
rather a decided and stern indifference
shone in her pensive and sharp eyes.
She was one of those
Roman beauties
that are rare even in Rome,

where one can never meet them
without a dumb wonder.
It was a great secret
of life in Rome
that made its appearance in the least
propitious place,
in its most dignified form.
Whence was coming, or whither was
going
the pretty Roman with her
shiny and curled hair?
What profession could one ascribe to
her?
Having shifted toward the door
she found someone to converse with
with familiarity.
And she was turning to me her shoul-
ders,
high like stretched wings.
At the Colosseo she alighted with
lightness,
vanishing from my eyes, alas, forever.

From the collection "Poesie Aggiunte," 1949, by Vincenzo Cardarelli.

Awaiting (Attesa)

Today that I was waiting, you did not come.
And I know what your absence says,
your absence was a tumultuous whirl,
in the emptiness you left behind,
like a star.
It says that you will not love me.
Like a Summer storm
that announces itself then recedes,
similarly you denied yourself to my thirst.
Love, when is born, has such sudden regrets.
Silently we understood each other.
Love, Love, as always,
I would offer you flowers and curses.

From the collection "Poesie," 1949, by Vincenzo Cardarelli.

Adolescent (Adolescente)

Upon you, virgin adolescent,
a sacred shadow seems to rest.
No thing is more mysterious
and adorable and proper
than your disrobed flesh.
Yet, you conceal yourself
under the mindful dress
and dwell far away
with your grace
where you know not who will reach you
there.
Certainly not me. When I see you passing
by
at such a regal distance,
with your locks unbound
and all your body shaft-like straight,
a vertigo sweeps me away.
You are the impenetrably smooth crea-
ture

in whose breathing is pressing
the obscure joy of a flesh that barely
bears its own plenitude.
In the blood, which on your face
has hues of flame,
the cosmos has its laughter
as in the black eye of a swallow.
Your pupil is burnt
by the sun within it.
Your mouth is closed tight.
Your white hands know not
the shameful perspiration of contacts.
And I think how your body
laborious and vague
despairs love
in the heart of man!

And yet someone will spoil the flower,
mouth that is a spring of fresh water.
Someone who will not even know it,
a fisherman of sponges,
shall have such a rare pearl.
It shall be a grace and a blessing
not to have sought you

and not to know who you are
and not to be able to relish you
with the subtle awareness
that offends the jealous God.
Oh yes, the animal will be
sufficiently unaware
so that he dies not before touching you.
And everything is so.
You too know not who you are.
And you shall let yourself be taken,
just to see how is the game played,
to laugh a bit together.
Like a flame loses itself in the light,
at the touch of reality
the mysteries that you promise
melt away into nothingness.
Not consumed, shall pass by
so much delight!
You will give yourself away, lose your-
self,
in the whims that can never guess
right, with the first one that you will fan-
cy.
Time loves the playfulness

that seconds it,
not the cautious wish that dallies.
In such a way does childhood
make the world tumble
and the wise is nothing but a boy
sorrowful because he has grown up.

From the collection "Prologhi," 1916, by Vincenzo Cardarelli.

A Biographical Note from the Author:

I grew up on the sunny hillsides of the Rhaetian Alps Mountains in Italy, where I spent a musing youth. Soon after graduating in Economics at the University of Milan, I set off to see the world, dwelling in London, Amsterdam, Barcelona, and in the USA — in NYC, Princeton and Philadelphia — working many years in the Online Publishing industry with The Wall Street Journal/Dow Jones Group.
Check out my literary work on my website: baruffi.me

Printed in Great Britain
by Amazon

32566465R00047